The Changing Shape of the Land

Written by Marilyn Woolley
Series Consultant: Linda Hoyt

WorldWise™
Content-based Learning

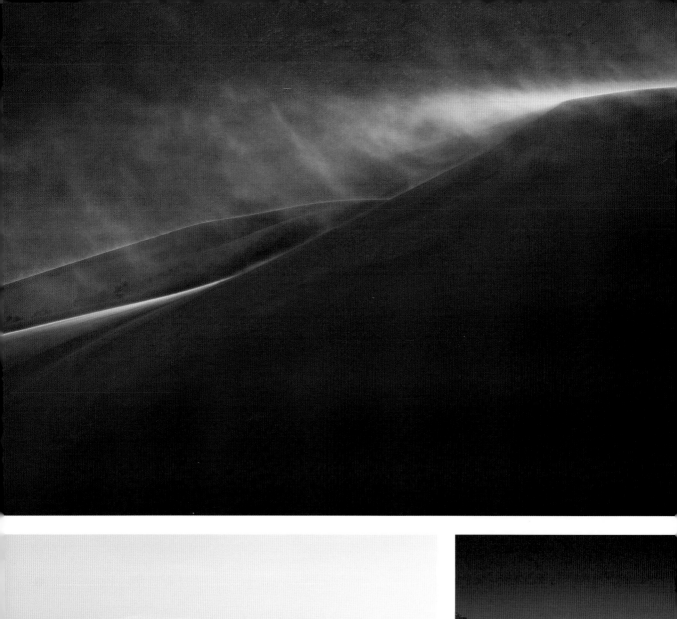

Contents

Introduction

The land around us is always changing. Water, wind, ice and snow can all change the shape of the land.

Water can wash soil, sand and bits of rock to other places. Wind can blow soil and sand to other places. Ice and snow can move down mountains.

When any of this happens, parts of the land are worn away and new shapes are made.

This is called **erosion**.

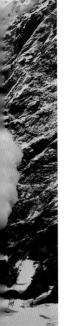

Chapter 1

Coastal erosion

Beaches, rocks and cliffs along a coastline can be changed by wind and water.

Beaches

Beaches are made of sand or small rocks that have been washed up on the beach.

Waves bring some sand from the bottom of the sea to the beach. Rivers carry sand with them as they flow to the sea. This sand is left on the beach when the river flows into the sea. Wind blows all of this sand into hills called sand dunes. The wind keeps changing the shape and size of sand dunes.

Water from waves or heavy rain keeps changing the shape of beaches. It washes sand and rocks back into the sea. The sand and rocks in this water carve out small holes in rocky platforms to make **rock pools**.

Tall rocks and cliffs

Waves, wind, sand and rain change the shape of rocks and cliffs.

Wind, rain and seawater blow or crash against rocks and cliffs along the coastline. This wears away rocks and cliffs.

Heavy rain can also make cracks in rocky cliffs. Part of the cliff can break away, and soil and rocks can fall down onto the beach. This changes the shape of the beach.

Mountain erosion

Ice and snow, as well as wind and rain can make new shapes on mountains and the land below them.

Glaciers

A glacier is like a river of ice.

When snow falls and the wind blows high up in the mountains, snow can pile up and turn into ice. The pile can become so heavy that the ice starts to move downhill. The moving ice is called a glacier.

Glacier

A glacier moves very slowly. The heavy ice tears off
rocks and makes big holes and valleys in the land.
When rain falls in these holes and valleys, a new lake
or river is made.

As the glacier moves down to where the weather is
warmer, it begins to melt. Large piles of rocks are
left where the glacier's ice has melted away.

Avalanche

Avalanches and landslides

Sometimes huge chunks of snow break away from the
side of a mountain or glacier and crash down to the
valley below. This is an **avalanche**.

Strong winds can start avalanches. An avalanche covers
everything in its path as it crashes down the mountain.

Heavy soil and rocks can also slide down a steep slope. This is a **landslide**. Heavy rain can cause landslides. Water washes away the soil, and this wet soil becomes a river of mud that moves very quickly downhill.

Find out more

Find out about avalanches and landslides that have occurred in your country.

Landslide

Desert erosion

Wind and water can make new shapes in rocky and sandy **deserts**. A desert is a place where there is not much rain.

Rocky deserts

In rocky deserts, wind blows sand and small rocks against larger rocks. The larger rocks wear away, and sometimes pieces of rock break off. This makes new rocky shapes in the desert.

When it does rain in the desert, water washes away sand and wears away rocks. This changes their shape.

Wind can also change the shape of rocks as it blows sand against them. The wind can blow away any small parts of the rocks that have broken off.

Sandy deserts

In sandy deserts, wind blows the sand around and makes large sand dunes.

When it rains in sandy deserts, water washes the sand away. It can make water holes, streams and small gullies.

Sandstorm

If there are trees or plants in the desert, these hold the sand in place. Without trees and plants, the sand is easily blown away.

Sometimes, strong winds blow for many days. The air is full of sand and it is very hard to see. This is a **sandstorm**.

Find out more

Where are the largest sand dunes in Australia? Find them on a map.

Conclusion

Erosion is caused by water, wind, ice and snow.

Water and wind blow or wash away soil, rocks and sand.

Glaciers move down mountains and tear away rocks and carry them to other places. **Avalanches** crash down mountains.

As a result of erosion, the shape of the land around us keeps changing.

Glossary

avalanche large amounts of snow, ice, rocks and soil suddenly and violently sliding down a mountain

deserts areas that have little available water

erosion the wearing away of the land by natural forces

landslide large amounts of soil and rocks suddenly sliding down a mountain

rock pools seawater that is left on the land after the tide goes out

sandstorm a storm where the winds blow huge amounts of sand into the air

Index

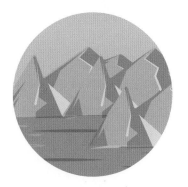